starts easy

gets harder!

Challenging picture puzzles

Over 75 timed puzzles to test your skills!

Illustrated by Giulia Lombardo, Marc Parchow,

Andrea Ebert, & Nicolae Negura

Text: Elizabeth Golding

Designed by Ben Potter & Anton Poitier

BARRON'S

First edition for the United States and Canada published in
2017 by Barron's Educational Series, Inc.

All inquiries should be addressed to:
Barron's Educational Series, Inc.
250 Wireless Boulevard
Hauppauge, NY 11788
www.barronseduc.com

ISBN: 978-1-4380-0979-7
Date of Manufacture: November 2016
Manufactured by: Shenzhen Caimei Printing Co, Ltd.,
Shenzhen, China
Printed in China
9 8 7 6 5 4 3 2 1

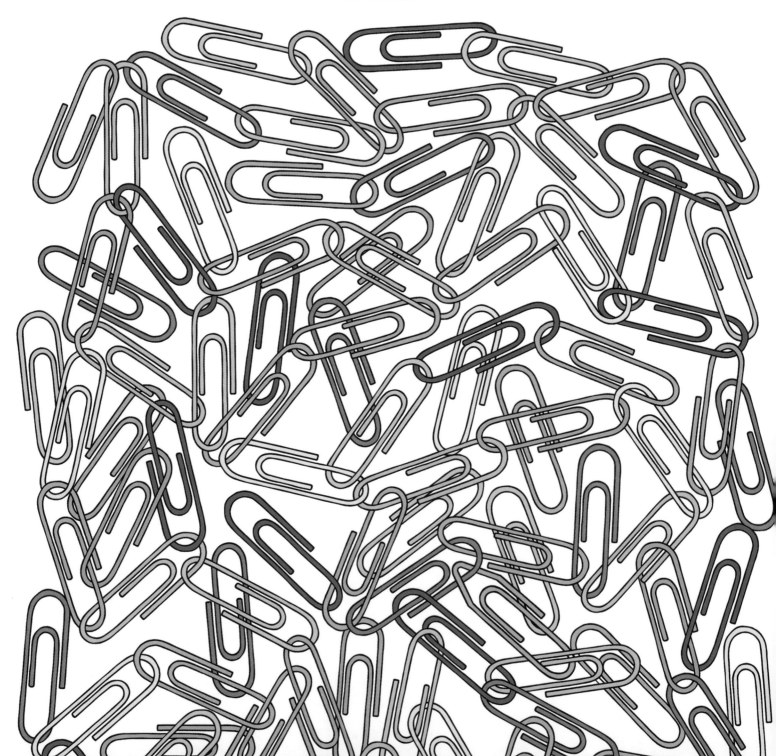

Puzzle fun!

This book is jam-packed with amazing picture puzzles that start easy and get harder as you go through the book. Every puzzle has a time challenge at the top of the page. See if you can solve the puzzle faster and beat the challenge. Look out for this symbol:

BEAT THIS!

Time challenge to beat.

The clock is in minutes and seconds. Use a watch with a second hand or a mobile phone timer to check your time from start to finish. You could write down your time on each page.

Solve and color!

If you like, you can also color the puzzles. Many of them are partially colored or blank, so you can complete the blank areas with colored pencils.

The answers are at the end of the book in case you get stuck!

On your mark, get set, go!

Which ball belongs with which piece of sports equipment?

Choose the three shapes below that complete the picture.

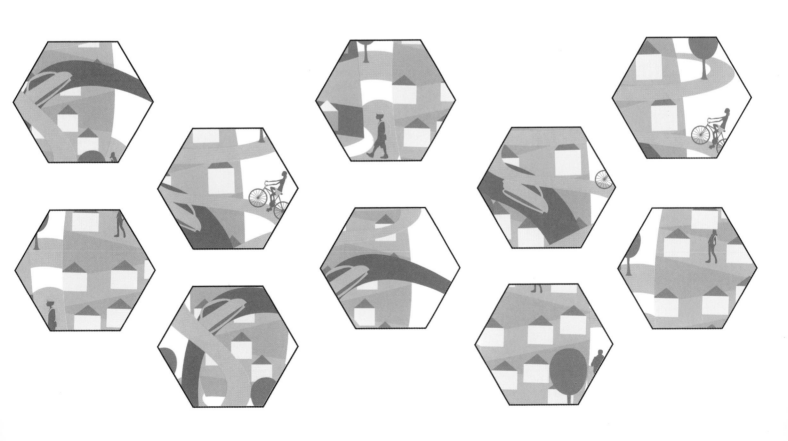

Help the dog through the streets to reach the bone.

The wolf has blown down the little pigs' house. There is one unexpected item. Can you find it?

How many animals can the giraffe see?

A caterpillar is hiding in this salad. Can you find it?

BEAT THIS!
01:00

Find the four-leaf clover!

One dog is the odd one out. Which one?

Only two penguins, crabs, and seals are the same. Circle them.

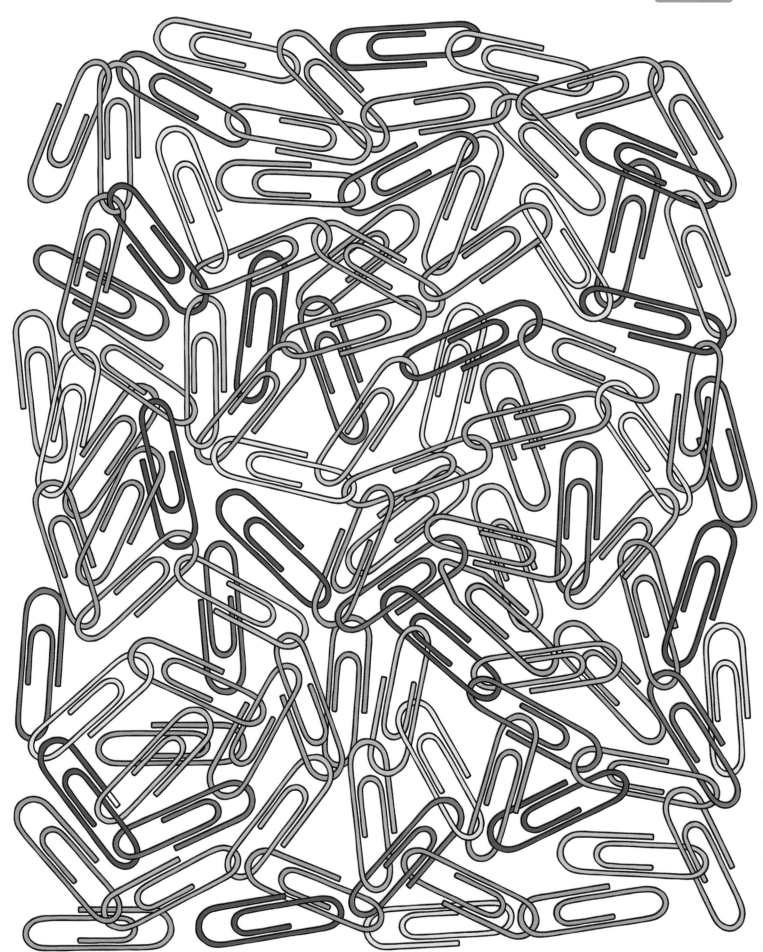

There are at least two of everything, except one thing!
Which is it?

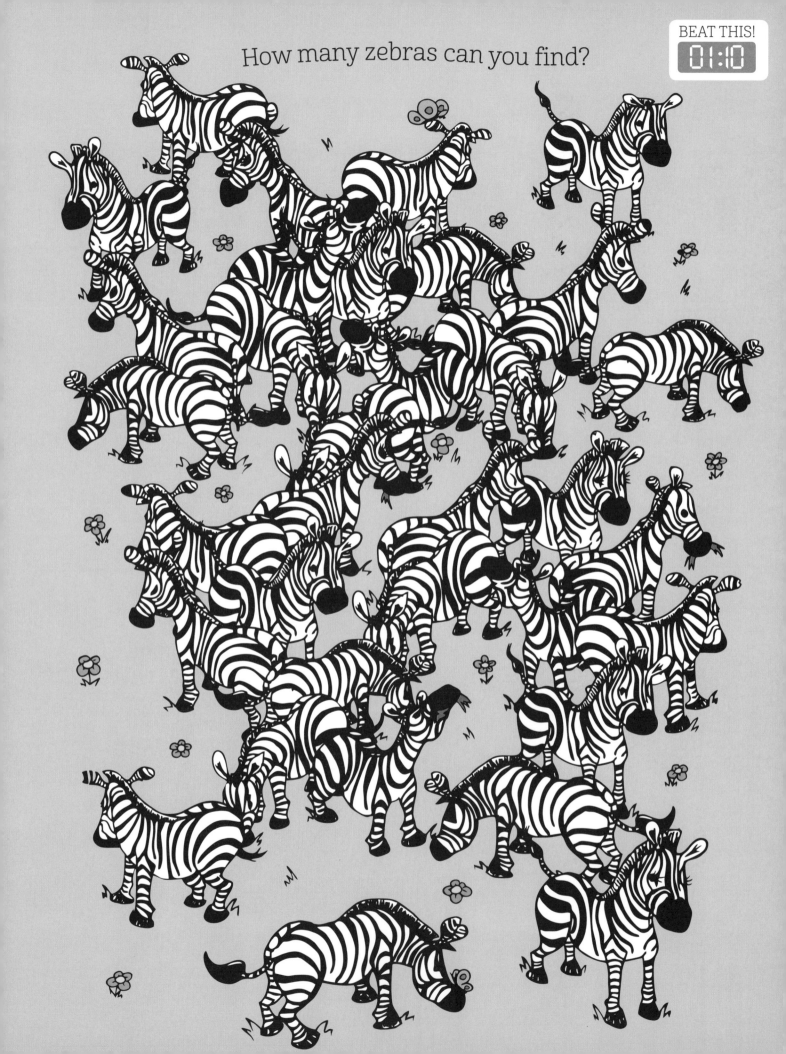

Find the puppy with
less than five spots.

Help the ant reach the Queen!

Find the objects that don't belong in the fridge.

Which pictures match what you can see in the two red circles?

Four cakes are different from the rest. Circle them.

BEAT THIS!
01:25

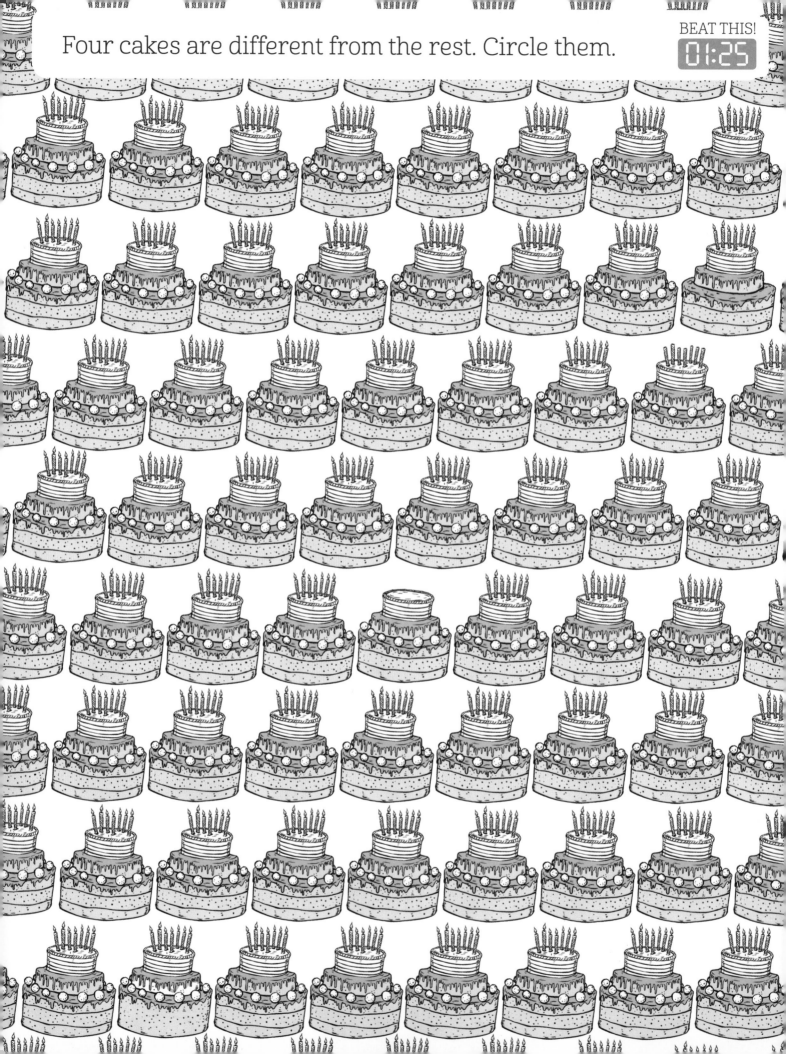

Match each dolphin to its shadow.

One instrument is out of place. Circle it then color the picture!

BEAT THIS!

Find the nine things that don't belong on the beach.

BEAT THIS!
01:30

How many green butterflies overlap with each other?

BEAT THIS!

01:30

Find the pencil sharpened at both ends!

You know who eats what! But who arrives first?

BEAT THIS! 01:45

Find the flamingo standing on one leg. Color them all!

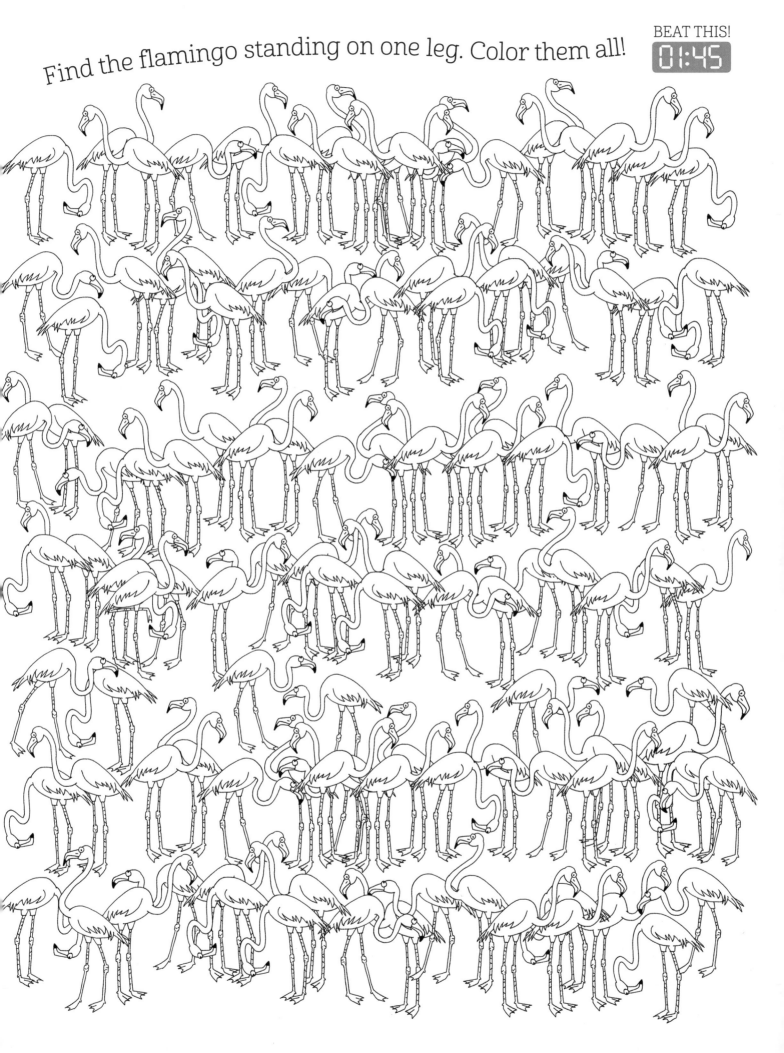

Jack has lost all his balloons! How many did he lose?

Find the three pairs of chairs.

Find the odd one out.

Only one of the arrows leads to the nectar.

Find the 12 things that don't belong in this room.

Find the six things that don't belong in this picture.

BEAT THIS!
01:45

CENTRAL STATION

10:00

Men's fashion@.com Fashion

COMPUTERS LAPTOPS

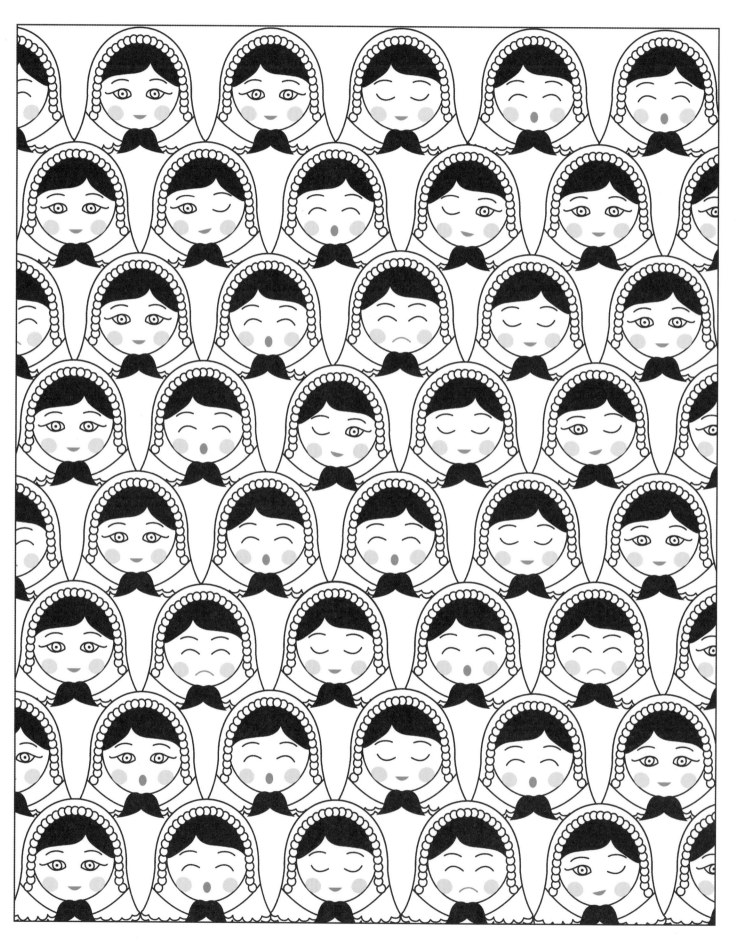

Find the farm animals.

How many starlings can you count?

One has something in its beak. Which one?

One paint splash is different from the rest. Which one?

How many little fish can you find?

Look at the shapes below.

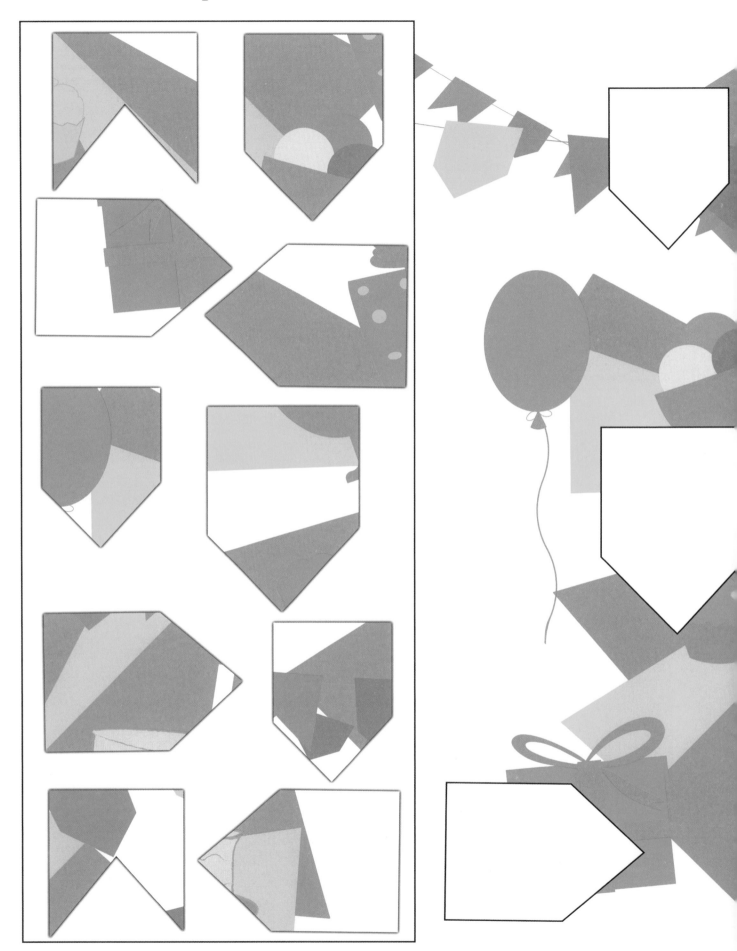

Only eight shapes will fit the picture. Which ones?

BEAT THIS!
01:55

One elephant is different. Which one? Why?

One panda is the odd one out. Which one?

BEAT THIS!
02:00

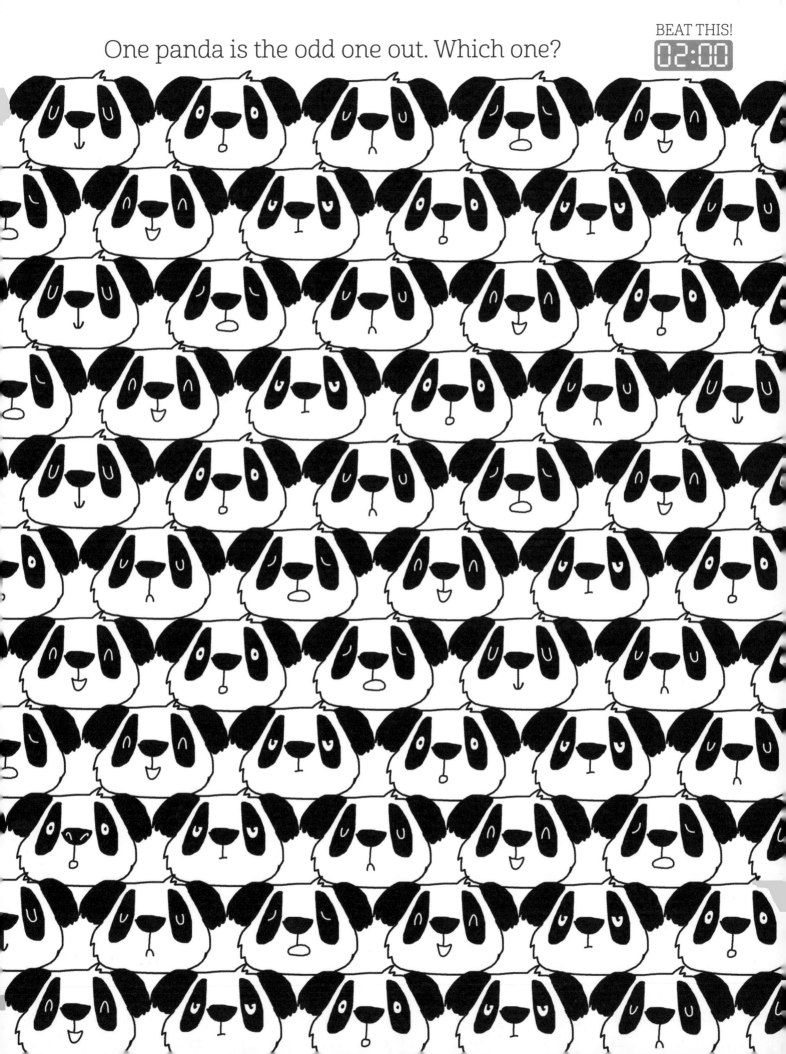

Match each animal to its shadow.

Which pirate ship found the most treasure?

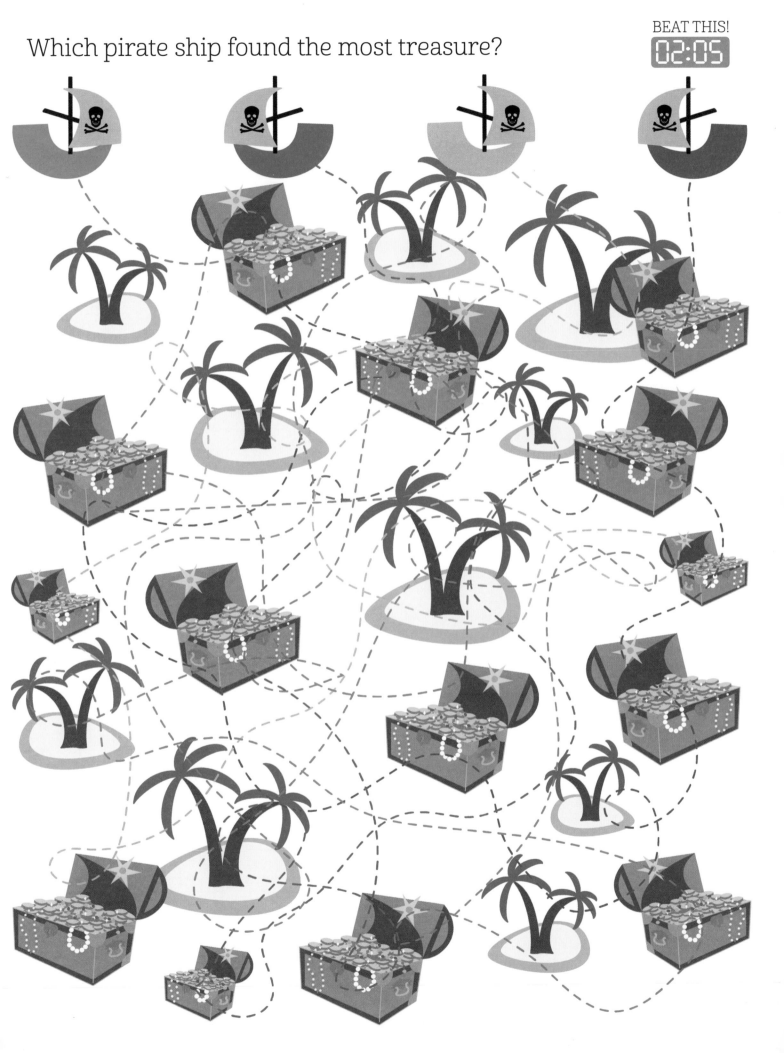

Two castles are identical. Which ones?

How many birds can you see? Color them in.

Only one set of blocks has nine different colors.
Which one?

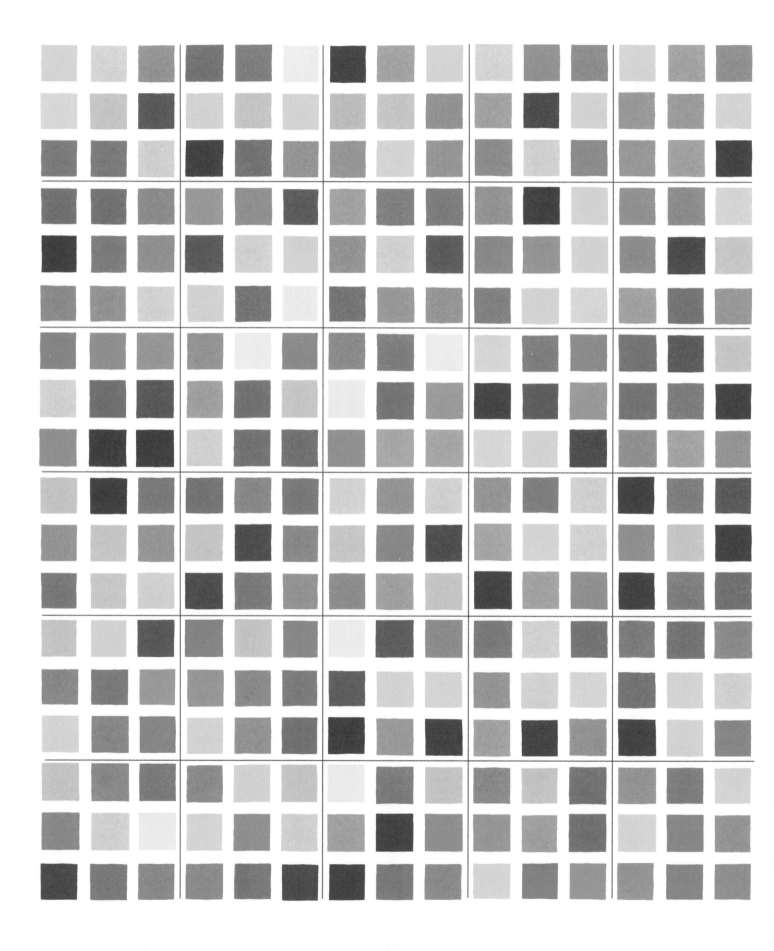

Katie has lost a button from her jacket.
Can you help her find it?

BEAT THIS!
02:30

Which duck laid the most eggs?

This tea set was smashed!
Match the broken pieces
to the original.

How many crabs can you find? Circle them.

How many stars can Sophie see from her window?

Two cats, two fish, and two mice are the same.
Which are they?

A spot on one of the leopards is wrong.
Where is it?

The chicken has lost two feathers. They're hiding in the picture! Can you find them?

How many triangles can you find? Color them in.

Sam and Joe are looking at the same cube.
Which one are they looking at?

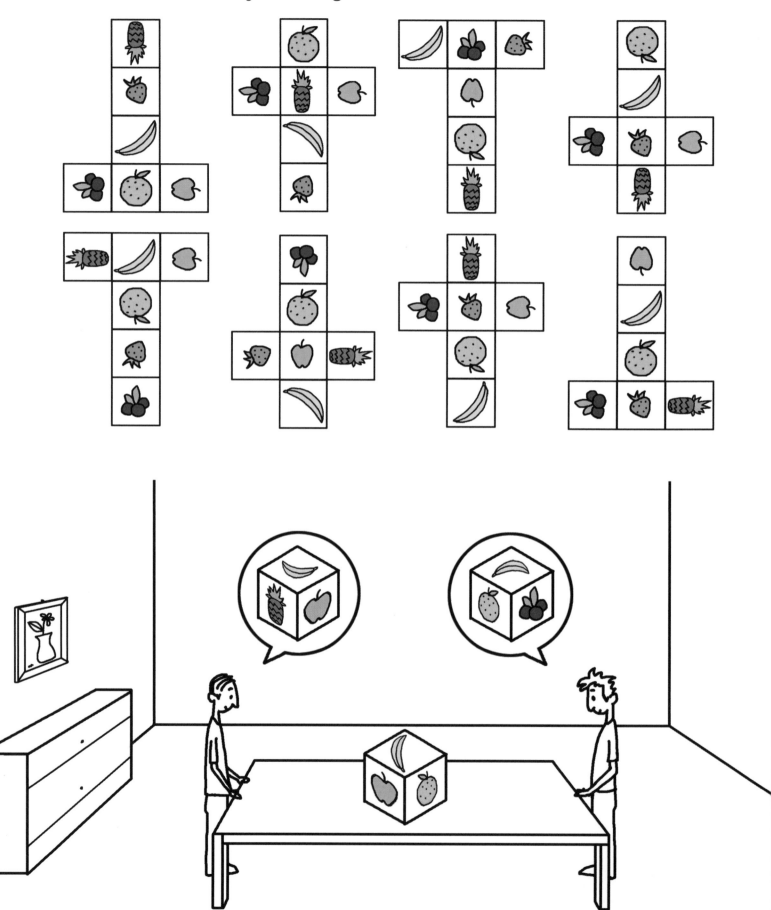

Four squares have exactly six shapes in them.
Find them and beat the clock!

Find the snail that's waiting to be found.
Color it in.

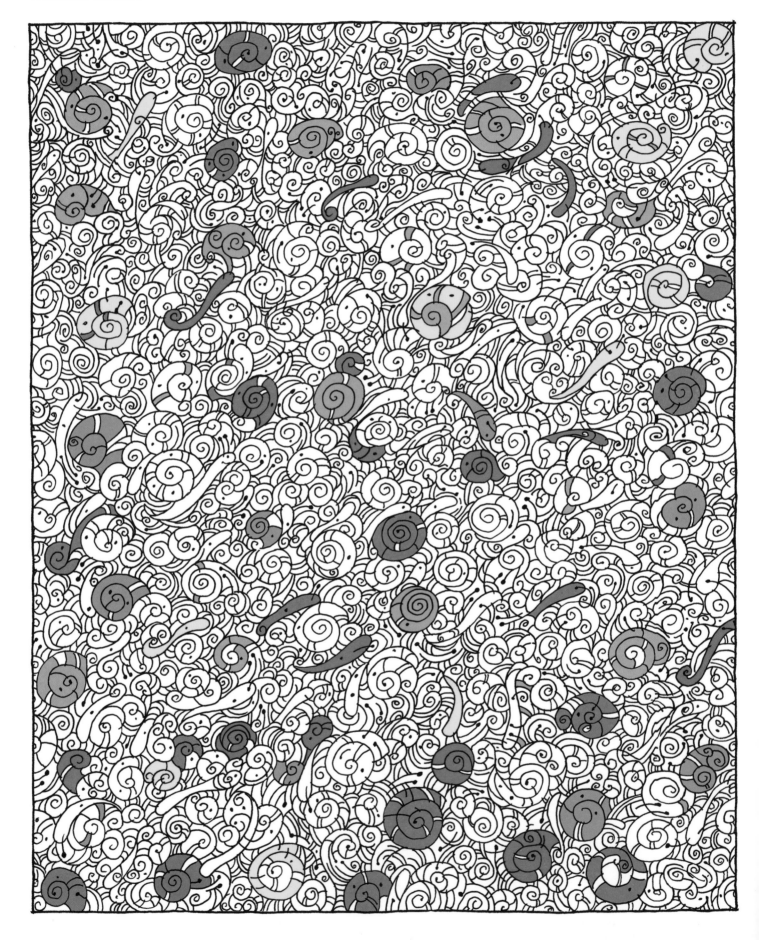

How many patches can you see on the giraffe's body?

Two snakes have no stripes. Where are they?

BEAT THIS!
03:30

Find these animals hidden in the ocean. There are 29 in total.

The bottom picture is jumbled. Spot 10 differences.

BEAT THIS!
03:40

Color the dots, diamonds, and crosses all different colors to discover which animal likes acorns.

Can you complete the squares to match the big picture?

Color in both the pictures!

Can you complete the squares to match the big picture?

Color in chameleons, with different colors!

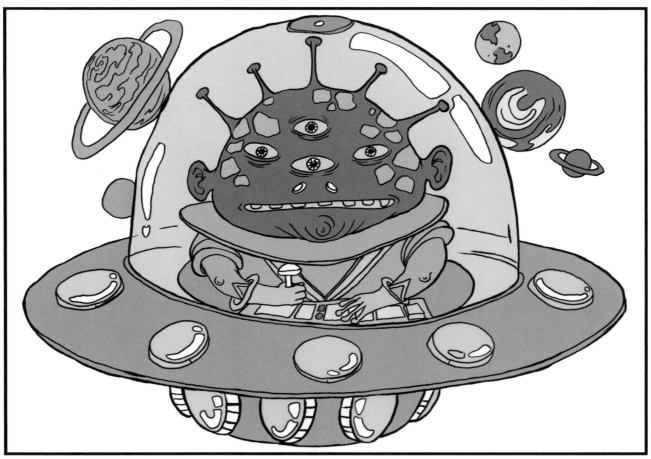

Can you copy the picture below to complete the squares?

This one is tricky because it's reversed!

There are two symmetrical stars hiding in this picture. Where are they?

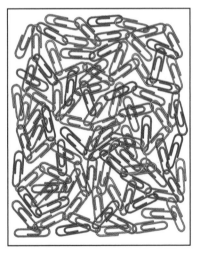

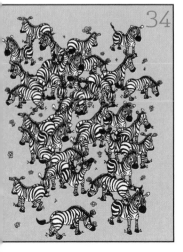

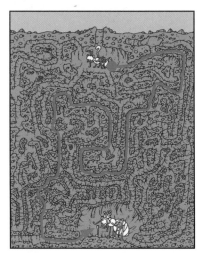
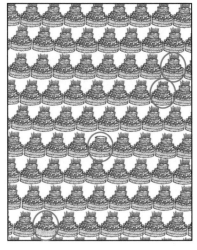
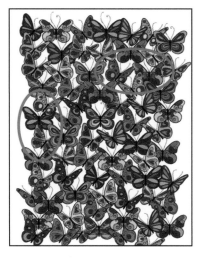
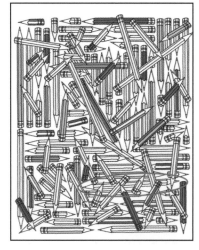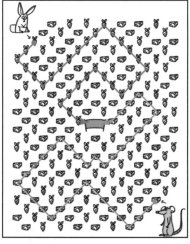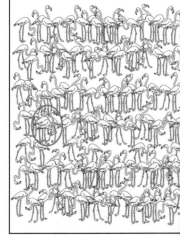

 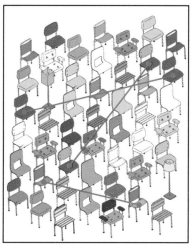  

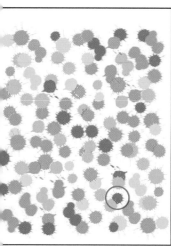  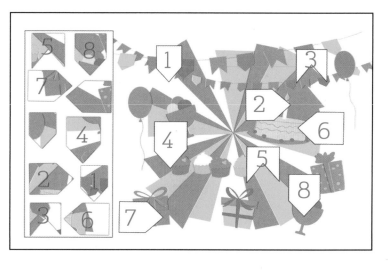

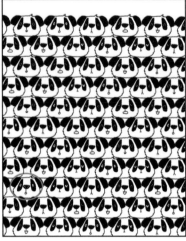

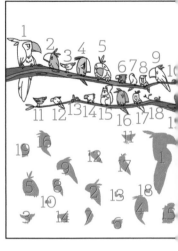

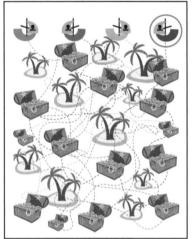
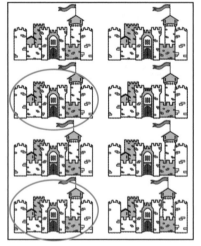

69

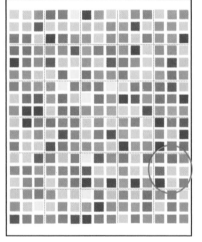

106

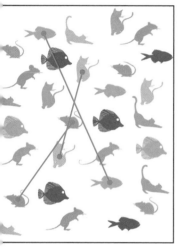
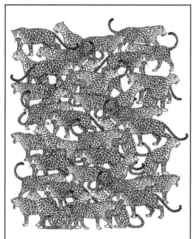

50

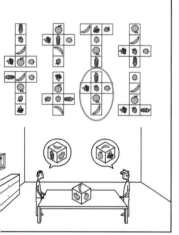

Colour them in.

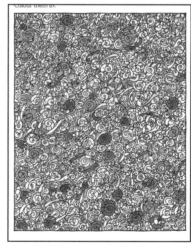

159

20

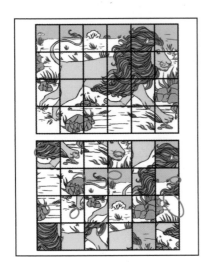